KAMALA HARRIS

★ ★ ★

Rooted in Justice

WRITTEN BY
NIKKI GRIMES

ILLUSTRATED BY
LAURA FREEMAN

Atheneum Books for Young Readers
NEW YORK LONDON TORONTO SYDNEY NEW DELHI

For Clarity Bates and Christopher Bates Jr., leaders in the making
—N. G.

To my parents, James and Trudy, whose strength and bravery created a family
—L. F.

ATHENEUM BOOKS FOR YOUNG READERS * An imprint of Simon & Schuster Children's Publishing Division * 1230 Avenue of the Americas, New York, New York 10020 * Text copyright © 2020 by Nikki Grimes * Illustrations copyright © 2020 by Laura Freeman * All rights reserved, including the right of reproduction in whole or in part in any form. * ATHENEUM BOOKS FOR YOUNG READERS is a registered trademark of Simon & Schuster, Inc. Atheneum logo is a trademark of Simon & Schuster, Inc. * For information about special discounts for bulk purchases, please contact Simon & Schuster Special Sales at 1-866-506-1949 or business@simonandschuster.com. * The Simon & Schuster Speakers Bureau can bring authors to your live event. For more information or to book an event, contact the Simon & Schuster Speakers Bureau at 1-866-248-3049 or visit our website at www.simonspeakers.com. * The text for this book was set in ITC Berkeley Oldstyle Std. * The illustrations for this book were rendered digitally. * Manufactured in the United States of America * 1220 LAK * 10 9 8 7 6 5 * Library of Congress Cataloging-in-Publication * Names: Grimes, Nikki, author. | Freeman, Laura, illustrator. * Title: Kamala Harris : rooted in justice / Nikki Grimes ; illustrated by Laura Freeman. * Description: First edition. | New York, New York : Atheneum Books for Young Readers, 2020. | Includes bibliographical references. | Audience: Ages 4–8 | Audience: Grades K–1 | Summary: "The first-ever picture book biography on Senator Kamala Harris"—Provided by publisher. * Identifiers: LCCN 2019059811 | ISBN 9781534462670 (hardcover) | ISBN 9781534462687 (eBook) * Subjects: LCSH: Harris, Kamala, 1964–—Juvenile literature. | Women legislators—United States—Biography—Juvenile literature. | Legislators—United States—Biography—Juvenile literature. | Women presidential candidates—United States—Biography—Juvenile literature. | Presidential candidates—United States—Biography—Juvenile literature. | United States. Congress. Senate—Biography—Juvenile literature. * Classification: LCC E901.1.H37 G75 2020 | DDC 328.73092 [B]—dc23 * LC record available at https://lccn.loc.gov/2019059811

Eve slammed the door when she got home from first grade. "Eve! You know we don't slam doors in this house," her mom said. "What's going on?"

"Teacher asked what we wanted to be when we grew up, and I said President, and Calvin said, 'Girls can't be President, stupid.'"

"Well, he's wrong," said her mother. "Girls can grow up to be President. In fact, a girl from right here in Oakland hopes to be President one day."

Life is a story
you write day by day.
Kamala's begins with a name
that means "lotus flower."
See how her beautiful smile
opens wide, like petals
fanning across the water's surface?
But you don't see the flower's roots. Her roots.
They grow deep, deep, deep down.
Let me show you.

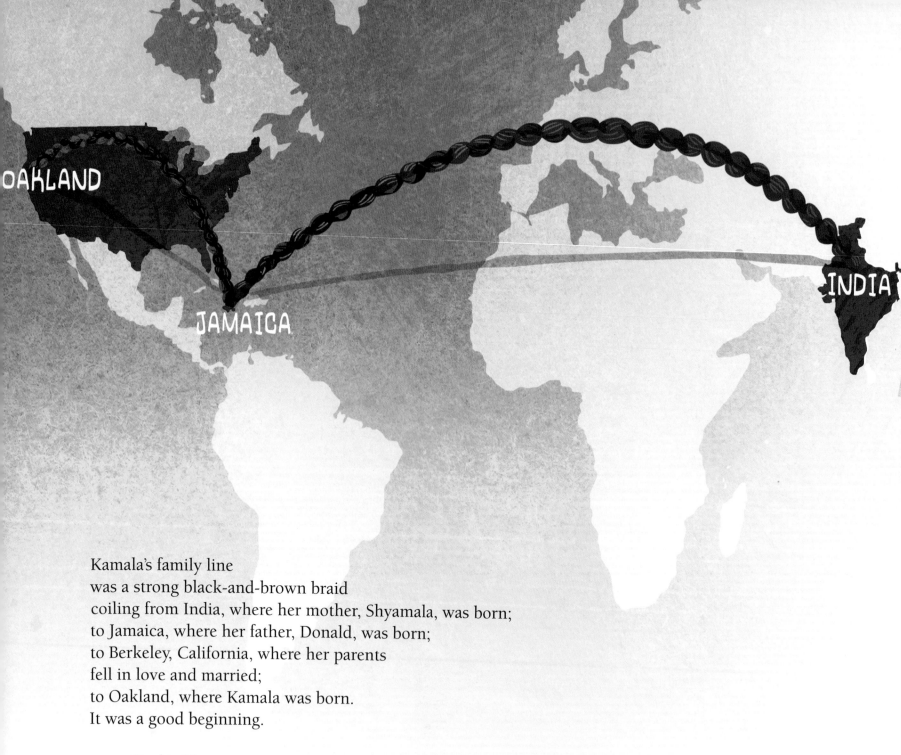

Kamala's family line
was a strong black-and-brown braid
coiling from India, where her mother, Shyamala, was born;
to Jamaica, where her father, Donald, was born;
to Berkeley, California, where her parents
fell in love and married;
to Oakland, where Kamala was born.
It was a good beginning.

"Is this like once upon a time?"
"Not exactly," said Eve's mom.
"This story is true."

Right away, Kamala was like clay
her parents molded for action.
When her mother wasn't
hunting cures for cancer,
and her father wasn't teaching,
both marched for civil rights
and went to lectures by
Dr. Martin Luther King Jr.
Kamala was right there, too,
bouncing along in her stroller,
chewing on her pacifier
and words like "peace" and "justice."

"What's justice?" Eve asked her mom.
"Justice is another word for fairness."

Once, when tiny Kamala was fussing,
her mother couldn't figure out
what was the matter.
"What do you want, little girl?" she asked.
"Freedom!" said Kamala,
and a waterfall of laughter
sputtered from her mother's mouth.
At demonstrations,
marchers often chanted,
"What do we want?"
and the answer was always
"Freedom!"
Little Kamala had been listening.

Kamala's baby sister, Maya,
screamed her way into the world
when Kamala was two.
In no time, the sisters were having
faraway adventures together,
like visiting their grandparents in Zambia.
Grandfather P. V. Gopalan
was a senior diplomat there.
He had once fought for
India's independence.
 His wife, Rajam, Kamala's grandmother,
 fought for the rights of women.

Little by little, on these visits,
Kamala and Maya learned that
fighting for justice
ran in the family.

Sadly, when Kamala was seven,
her family squeezed into a different shape.
Her parents divorced,
and her daddy moved to Palo Alto
while Mommy and the girls packed for "the flatlands,"
the black working-class area in Berkeley.
Having a long-distance daddy
can make your heart hurt,

but Kamala's new neighbors
welcomed her family
with smiles and helping hands,
warm as sunshine. Still,
Kamala was sometimes lonely for her daddy.
Luckily, her godmother, Aunt Mary,
lived close by and gave Kamala extra hugs
whenever she needed them.

Like other black and brown kids in the flatlands,
Kamala was part of a California program
to integrate the schools.
Every day, she rode a yellow bus,
bumping through familiar city streets,
all the way to the wealthy, white part of town
with sprawling hillsides,
painted with gardens.
Thousand Oaks Elementary
was a world away,
but Kamala didn't mind.
There, she got to meet kids who were
rich and poor, black and white;
kids who celebrated holidays
she'd never even heard of.
There, teachers taught her
to count to ten in many different languages.

*"Ooh! I can count to ten in
Spanish!" said Eve.
"Who taught you that?"
asked her mom.
"Guadalupe, from next door."
Eve smiled proudly.*

School let out before Mrs. Harris got home,
so Kamala and Maya spent the afternoons
at the Shelton house two doors down,
where Mrs. Regina Shelton ran
day-care and after-school programs
with posters on the wall of Frederick Douglass,
Sojourner Truth, and Harriet Tubman.
Mrs. Shelton was a second mother to Kamala,
always encouraging her to have confidence.

Once, Mrs. Shelton bit into a lemon bar
Kamala had made all by herself,
accidentally using salt instead of sugar.
"Oh! Delicious!" said Mrs. Shelton.
"Maybe a little too much salt,
but really delicious," she said,
never pointing out Kamala's total failure.
That day, Mrs. Shelton let Kamala walk away
feeling successful, feeling like
she could do anything.

After school, Kamala's days
bulged with busyness.
She had homework, piano lessons,
ballet classes, and Barbie playtime.
Thursday nights were the best, though.
The family would go to the Rainbow Sign,
a cultural center celebrating
black art, music, books, and film.
James Baldwin spoke there,
Maya Angelou read there,
and Nina Simone sang there.

Nina's gravelly voiced version of
"To Be Young, Gifted and Black"
often rang through Kamala's home.
The more she heard this favorite song,
the more Kamala thought,
I'm young, gifted, and black, too.

On Sundays,
when they weren't visiting their father,
Kamala and Maya rocked from side to side
at the 23rd Avenue Church of God,
where they tapped tambourines and sang
as part of the children's choir.
"Fill My Cup, Lord" was Kamala's favorite hymn.
The church was where she learned the Bible,
that God asks us to speak up for those who can't,
to defend the rights of the poor and needy,
like some lawyers do.
Her uncle Sherman was that kind of lawyer.
Maybe someday Kamala could be one, too.

"I don't want to be a lawyer," said Eve.
"But I like making sandwiches for the homeless.
That's helping too, right?"
"Right," said her mom.

In her first year of middle school,
Kamala would need a lot of faith.
She learned a new lesson about change,
a lesson dressed in down jackets and mittens:
Her family was moving north,
where twelve feet of snow
and her mother's new job waited in Montréal.
"It will be a wonderful adventure,"
Shyamala told her girls,
but Kamala grumbled.
The thought of leaving her friends
and the warmth of sunny California
made her shiver.

It was February, and Montréal,
robed in winter's sparkling white,
felt like it had ice in its veins.
Kamala couldn't stop shivering.
Worse yet, their new neighbors
spoke French, a language Kamala's mother
insisted her daughters learn.
The English name of the French school
her mother handpicked for them was
"Our Lady of the Snows."

"That's a funny name," said Eve.
"Maybe," said her mom. "But Kamala wasn't laughing."

Montréal was no place for a lotus flower.
Sighing, Kamala unpacked her new clothes
and her old experiences—
like marching for change with her mom.
One spring day, when the temperature
rose enough for outdoor sports,
Kamala and Maya marched
in front of their apartment building,
waving picket signs because kids
weren't allowed to play soccer
on the front lawn.
It wasn't fair, and Kamala
cared a lot about fairness.
The building manager read Kamala and Maya's signs
and changed the rules.

Kamala adjusted to life in Canada,
but memories of her home country
still rang her heart like a bell.
After graduating high school,
she ached to return to America,
where her parents had nursed her
on the Civil Rights Movement.
She couldn't wait to follow
in the footsteps of her heroes:
Constance Baker Motley,
Charles Hamilton Houston,
and Thurgood Marshall.
Marshall had attended Howard University,
and Kamala decided she would, too.

On her first day at Howard,
Kamala turned this way and that,
smiling at the faces of students from
America, Africa, the Caribbean—
it was Thursday nights at the Rainbow Sign
all over again, where everyone in the room
was black, like her.
They reminded her of home
and the people she wanted to help,
the people she wanted to fight for.
This university would begin to teach her how.

Howard seemed like a perfect place
to run her very first campaign.
It was for class representative of
the Liberal Arts Student Council.
Her competition was tough,
but so was Kamala.
Every day, between classes,
she passed out flyers in the campus yard
and told any students who'd listen
why they should vote for her.
When the last ballot was counted,
Kamala came out the winner.

"Daddy says I don't have any competition,
   'cause there's only one me," said Eve.
"That's right," said her mom.
"He should tell Kamala there's only one her."
   Eve's mom just smiled.

Kamala's time at Howard
was focused on the future.
She competed on the debate team
to sharpen her speaking skills,
she interned at the Federal Trade Commission,
she did research at the National Archives
to study the workings of government,

and on weekends, she joined fellow students
on the National Mall in Washington, DC,
to protest apartheid in South Africa.
Kamala was preparing to be
a woman warrior.

"Like Wonder Woman?" asked Eve.
"No. Better," said her mom.
"Wonder Woman isn't real."

Nothing matched the magic
of her second summer break,
when Kamala stepped through the doors
of the private Senate subway
as an intern for Senator Alan Cranston.
Kamala could barely hold in
the secret of her joy!
What could be better than
learning from someone
whose footsteps echoed
in the halls of power every day?

After Howard, California called Kamala home
to study at Hastings College of the Law.
Court cases and contracts filled Kamala's mind,
but changing lives filled her heart.
Elected President of the
Black Law Students Association,
Kamala invited major law firms to a job fair
so that more black graduates
had a fair chance to be hired
by the best companies in the country.
This work was great practice
for Kamala's future.

NOW
HIRING

Graduating law school meant there was one more exam to take:
the California Bar. Without passing it, Kamala could not practice the law.
She didn't pass, which taught Kamala something new: failure.
It is the toughest teacher, but it can also be the best
because it makes you dig down deep and try harder.

On the second try,
Kamala passed!

"If at first you don't succeed . . . ,"
said Eve's mom.
"Try, try again," finished Eve.

Kamala was finally ready to climb
the mountain of her dreams:
First, Deputy District Attorney.
Next, the first female
District Attorney of San Francisco.
Then, the first black woman
Attorney General of California.
Peak by peak, she rose,
eventually becoming
the second black woman
voted into the US Senate.
Lawyer, prosecutor, Senator—
the little girl named "lotus flower"
had turned herself into a person
others could call on for help.

"Did she use magic to turn herself into that
person?" asked Eve.
"No, sweetie. Kamala just used hard work."

As Senator, Kamala fought for laws
to help workers earn more money,
joined the Women's March on Washington
for equality and civil rights,
and telephoned lawyers
to help immigrant children
who came to America
looking for someplace safe to live.
Each time she answered a call for help,
Kamala proved that
her family's legacy of public service
was alive and well in her.

"What's a legacy?" asked Eve.
"It's like the inheritance you leave behind
for your children."

Kamala had traveled far,
but she hadn't finished climbing
the mountain of her dreams.
On Martin Luther King Jr.'s birthday,
on the TV show *Good Morning America*,
Kamala told the world,
"I'm running for President
of the United States."

SENATOR KAMALA HARRIS LIV
RISING DEMOCRATIC STAR ANNOUNCES

She immediately got goose bumps
wondering if Shirley Chisholm,
the first black woman to run for President,
was smiling down from heaven
that very moment!

Months into the race,
Kamala realized that running for President
cost more money than she thought,
and Kamala's campaign team
didn't have enough.
She decided to give up her run
for the 2020 presidential nomination.

*"That's okay," said Eve. "If at first
    you don't succeed, try, try again."*
"Exactly," said her mom.

The Senator's sadness lifted, though,
when a soft-spoken man named Joe
invited her to be his running mate.
And after a hard-fought campaign,
Kamala won an historic new name:
Madam Vice President!

Will Donald and Shyamala's daughter
get to be President herself someday?
Only God knows.
Kamala Harris is still writing
her American story.

And so are you.

"I know what happens next," said Eve.

"What?" asked her mom.

"Tomorrow, I'll tell Calvin that he's wrong, and he's a doofus!"

"Eve Temple, I taught you better than that," said her mother.

"Okay," said Eve, her fingers crossed behind her back.

"I won't tell him."

TIME LINE

1964 Born October 20 in Oakland, California, to Shyamala Gopalan, PhD, graduate of UC Berkeley, breast cancer researcher; and Donald Harris, UC Berkeley graduate, economics professor.

1969–1970 Parents separate.

1971 Kamala's mother files for divorce, moves Kamala and her younger sister, Maya, to Berkeley's "flatlands" area.

1976 Mother moves family to Montréal to accept a lucrative job offer while Kamala is in middle school. There, Kamala is forced to learn French.

1982 Kamala graduates from high school and returns to the United States to study at Howard University.

1986 Enters University of California Hastings College of the Law.

1988 Wins summer internship at Alameda County Superior Court, Oakland, California. This experience firmly sets her on a path to seek and pursue justice as a prosecutor.

1989 Graduates from University of California Hastings College of the Law.

1990 Is admitted to the State Bar of California.

1990–1998 Serves as Deputy District Attorney, Alameda County, California.

2004–2011 Serves as District Attorney of San Francisco, the city's first female elected to the post. Her mother addresses the crowd during the campaign kickoff.

2009 Shyamala Harris, Kamala's mother and single biggest influence, dies of colon cancer.

2011 Harris becomes the first Black woman elected Attorney General of California.

2012 Harris gives address at Democratic National Convention.

2014 Marries attorney Douglas Emhoff. (No one should be surprised that Emhoff was from a different race and culture. Diversity was the Gopalan-Harris family's middle name.)

2015 Declares candidacy for US Senate, vying for the seat of Barbara Boxer.

2016 Becomes the second Black woman to win a seat in the US Senate, representing California.

2019 On January 21, Martin Luther King Jr.'s birthday, Harris announces her bid for the 2020 presidential election. She chooses the campaign slogan "Kamala Harris for the People."

2019 On December 3, Harris withdraws from the 2020 presidential race for lack of sufficient funding.

2020 On August 11, Harris rejoins the 2020 presidential race as Joe Biden's chosen Democratic running mate.

2020 On November 7, Joe Biden wins the 2020 presidential election, and Kamala Harris becomes the first female, the first Black, and the first South Asian Vice President-elect of the United States. "While I may be the first woman in this office," says Harris, "I will not be the last."

SOURCES

Harris, Kamala. *Superheroes Are Everywhere*. New York, Philomel Books, 2019.

———. *The Truths We Hold: An American Journey*. New York, Penguin Press, 2019.

McNamee, Gregory Lewis. "Kamala Harris, United States Senator." *Encyclopaedia Britannica*, nd, britannica.com/biography/Kamala -Harris.

Nittle, Nadra Kareem. "Biography of California Senator Kamala Harris." ThoughtCo, nd, thoughtco.com/california-attorney -general-kamala-harris-2834885.

"Harris, Kamala Devi—Biographical Information" *Biographical Directory of the United States Congress*, nd, bioguideretro.congress .gov/Home/MemberDetails?memIndex=H001075.